PLANTS

by
Gemma McMullen

Photocredits

Abbreviations: l–left, r–right, b–bottom, t–top, c–centre, m–middle.

Front Cover – de2marco. 2 – Iakov Kalinin. 4l – homydesign. 4ml – irin–k. 4mr – Africa Studio. 4r – MJ Prototype. 4bl – Anan Kaewkhammul. 5tr – Maksym Bondarchuk. 5m – AnglianArt. 5b – Rich Carey. 6t – Reha Mark. 6b – varuna. 7t – Jaromir Chalabala. 7m – Tim UR. 7b – gkrphoto. 8t – Filipe B. Varela. 8b – Glasscage. 9t – Lukas Gojda. 9b – TunedIn by Westend61. 10t – Tischenko Irina . 10b – Zoltan Major. 11t – Furtseff. 11b – Anibal Trejo. 12t – wk1003mike. 12bl – Kucher Serhii. 12bm – LI CHAOSHU. 12br – PIYA PALAPUNYA. 13t – Tim UR. 13mt – Hong Vo. 13mb – TunedIn by Westend61. 13b – COBRASoft. 14 – Lightspring. 15tl – Victeah. 15tr – Le Do. 15b – isak55. 16t – Be Good. 16b – Nattapol Sritongcom. 17tl – SOMMAI. 17ml – Binh Thanh Bui. 17bl – Egor Rodynchenko. 17tr – Hong Vo. 17br – zcw. 18t – Barbol. 18 – Sergio33. 18l – irin–k. 19t – Reluk. 19b – happymay. 20 – aekikuis. 21t – Peter Zijlstra. 21b – Maya Kruchankova. 22t – hans.slegers. 22m – sydeen. 22bl – Sergey Peterman. 22bc – Hong Vo. 22br – Elsa Hoffmann. 23t – Madlen. 23m – Denis Tabler. 23b – D7INAMI7S. 24t – Iryna Denysova. 24b – Zhukov. 25t – Martina Roth. 25rt – Nattika. 25tm – Anna Sedneva. 25rb – topseller. 25lt – ConstantinosZ. 25lb – bergamont. 26t – Robyn Mackenzie. 26tr – Jiri Hera. 26br – surassawadee. 26bl – Zeljko Radojko. 26tl – pkproject. 27t – Brian A Jackson. 27b – stocker1970. 28t – Bonnie Taylor Barry. 28bl – Jenny Cottingham. 28br – IanRedding. 29tr – Sergey Chirkov. 29ml – JIANG HONGYAN. 29b – Iakov Kalinin. 30tl – Tukaram Karve. 30tr – Alexandra Lande. 30b – Madlen.

Images are courtesy of Shutterstock.com. With thanks to Getty Images, Thinkstock Photo and iStockphoto.

©2017
Book Life
King's Lynn
Norfolk PE30 4LS

ISBN: 978-1-78637-060-0

Written by:
Gemma McMullen

Edited by:
Grace Jones

Designed by:
Drue Rintoul

CONTENTS

Words in **bold** are explained in the glossary on page 31.

WHAT IS
A PLANT?

A plant is a living thing and, like all living things, plants need food and water in order to live and grow. Plants rely on natural water supplies for their water, but are able to make their own food using sunlight and air.

PLANTS COME IN MANY SHAPES AND SIZES.

LIFE-GIVING?

Plants are found all over planet Earth. Different plants are able to survive in **varying** conditions. Without plants, there would be little life on our planet. Plants provide food for animals and release **oxygen** into the **atmosphere**.

THE PARTS OF A PLANT

Though plants grow in many different forms, there are certain parts that they all have in common. Most plants are flowering plants. Flowering plants all have roots, a stem, leaves and flowers. A horse chestnut tree is a flowering plant and so is a buttercup.

A HORSE CHESTNUT TREE

A BUTTERCUP

NON-FLOWERING PLANTS

There are some plants which do not produce flowers. Seaweed (an algae) and moss are both examples of non-flowering plants. Non-flowering plants make new plants from spores rather than seeds.

SEAWEED

THE ROOTS

WHAT ARE ROOTS?

Roots are the anchor which hold a plant in the ground. The size of the roots is dependent on the size of the plant which they are anchoring. Most roots grow under the ground, making them difficult to see. They can spread far and wide and can become tangled amongst other roots. Large roots can become troublesome and have been known to lift pavements and damage brick walls!

ROOTS

GRASS WITHSTANDING STRONG WINDS AND HEAVY RAIN

THE ROLE OF AN ANCHOR

The roots, being the plant's anchor, keep the plant firmly in place. This is important during bad weather. Without roots, plants could be blown away by strong winds or washed away by heavy rain. As long as the roots are not damaged, the other plant parts can usually survive.

DAMAGED ROOTS

Roots are complicated systems. Plants can survive with minor damage to their roots, but if the damage is severe then the plant will **perish**. It is important to take great care when repotting or moving plants.

A PLANT BEING REPOTTED

ABSORBING WATER

Roots have another extremely important job. They **absorb** water and nutrients from the soil. Without water and nutrients, a plant would not be able to grow and survive.

HOW DO ROOTS DO IT?

Roots have tiny little hairs on them called root hairs. The root hairs are responsible for absorbing the water and nutrients from the ground. The water then needs to be **transported** upwards to the rest of the plant, so that it can be used where it is needed.

ROOTS

ROOT HAIRS

EDIBLE ROOTS

Humans can eat some plants' roots. A carrot is actually the root of a plant. Some plants have one large, **dominant** root called a tap root. A carrot is a tap root, meaning that it is the main root of its plant. There are also other, smaller roots as well as the tap root.

TAP ROOT

SMALLER ROOTS

Other tap roots that we eat include radishes, parsnips and celeriac. Sweet potatoes are root vegetables, but they are not tap roots.

RADISHES

PARSNIP

THE STEM

STEM

One of the main functions of the stem is to support the plant and to stop it from falling over. Most stems grow upwards out of the ground, but some stems can actually grow underneath the ground. Stems can be very large; the trunk of a tree is the main stem of the plant. Stems are usually straight and strong. Like the roots, one of their main functions is to keep the plant securely in one place.

THE TRUNK OF A TREE IS THE STEM OF THE PLANT.

WHAT ELSE DOES THE STEM DO?

The stem is the central **pillar** of the plant and is connected to all other parts of the plant. It supports any leaves and flowers (as well as the branches of larger plants) and transports water and nutrients upwards from the roots.

THE STEM SUPPORTS THE OTHER PLANT PARTS.

STORING WATER

The stem is also able to store water. Cactus plants naturally grow in hot climates, such as deserts. The stems of cacti store water in order to help the plants survive long periods without rain.

GROWING STEMS

The stem is usually the first part of a growing plant that we see above the ground. We call this growing stem a shoot and it actually contains leaves and flowers too.

USING STEMS

Stems can be used to make many things. Tree trunks, in particular, are used for logs, firewood and to make furniture such as chairs. The **pulp** from tree trunks is also used as one the materials needed to make paper. Parts of some plant stems are even used when making medicines.

PULP USED TO MAKE PAPER

FIREWOOD

LOGS

EDIBLE STEMS

Some plant stems are edible. Plant stems, such as those from asparagus and celery, are popular food choices. The stems of rhubarb plants can be used as part of desserts such as rhubarb crumble. Be careful though! The leaves of the plant are actually poisonous when eaten.

CELERY

ASPARAGUS

RHUBARB

THE ANIMALS ARE AT IT TOO!

Humans are not the only ones to find plant stems tasty. This panda is eating the stem of a bamboo grass. Pandas eat between 9 and 18 kilograms of bamboo every single day!

13

THE LEAVES

Plant leaves come in many shapes, sizes and even colours. The size of a leaf is not always dependent on the size of the plant. A large tree, for example, may not have particularly big leaves, but instead could have many smaller leaves. The leaves of a plant always grow above the surface of the ground. They are found along and above the plant's stem and are spread out in a way that makes sure that they receive as much sunlight as possible.

THE LEAVES TRY TO FACE THE SUN.

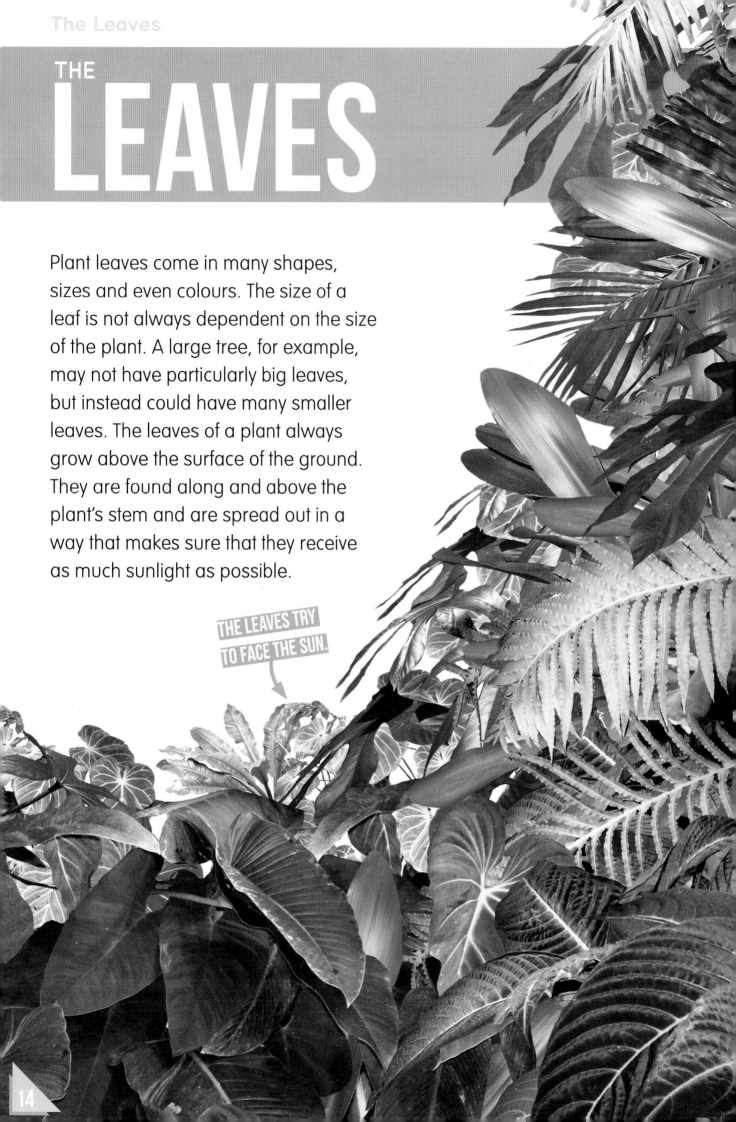

USING SUNLIGHT

Leaves are possibly the most important part of any plant because they are responsible for making a plant's food. Not only do the leaves **sustain** their own plant, but they also help to give life to other living things.

PHOTOSYNTHESIS

The leaf uses water, carbon dioxide (which is found in the air around us), chlorophyll (the part of the plant which makes it green) and light from the sun to make food for the plant. This process is called photosynthesis.

GIVING LIFE

As well as making sure that the plant survives, the leaves also help other living things to stay alive. Humans are not able to use the carbon dioxide which they breathe in. The leaves absorb carbon dioxide from the atmosphere and release oxygen back into the atmosphere. This benefits human life as we have more oxygen to breathe in.

LOSING WATER

Leaves lose a lot of the plant's water in the form of water vapour. It is very important that the roots are able to absorb plenty of water from the soil to replace the water lost through the leaves.

EDIBLE LEAVES

Some leaves can be eaten as part of a healthy diet. Lettuce leaves are the base of many salads and the leaves of cabbages and sprouts can be eaten as vegetables. Spinach and kale leaves are also popular vegetables.

Although the stems of celery plants are more commonly eaten, the leaves of celery plants can be eaten too. This is also true for the leaves of broccoli and cauliflower plants, despite their stems and flowers being more commonly eaten.

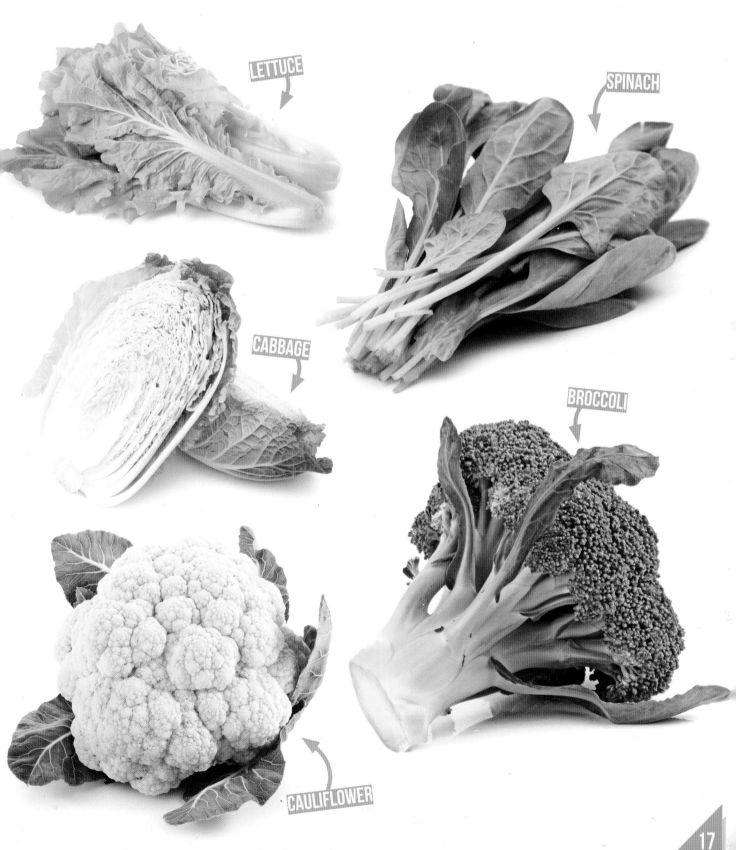

LETTUCE

SPINACH

CABBAGE

BROCCOLI

CAULIFLOWER

THE FLOWERS

All flowering plants grow flowers. They come in many different shapes and sizes. Grasses, shrubs and all trees, except conifers, produce flowers. Even cacti plants produce flowers. Flowers are important because they produce the seeds from which new plants can grow.

Flowers are quite **complex** things and each part of the flower has an important job to do. Many flowers are colourful and have a strong scent. This is to attract insects and birds.

CACTUS PLANT

THE PARTS OF A FLOWER

The petals of a flower are usually bright and colourful. Insects and birds are attracted to bright colours and so will visit the flower. Once there, they will drink nectar from the flower. In return for the sweet and sugary nectar, these creatures help flowers to **reproduce** by spreading pollen.

POLLEN

Pollen must travel from one flower to another of the same species in order to **fertilise** it. Pollen is made in the male part of a flower and needs to travel to the female part of a flower in order to reproduce.

A FLOWER CANNOT FERTILISE ITSELF, EVEN THOUGH IT HAS BOTH MALE AND FEMALE PARTS.

REPRODUCTION

Egg cells called ovules are found in the flower's ovary. Out of the ovary grows a style and at the end of the style is a stigma. The stigma is sticky to touch, so that pollen from other plants will easily stick to it.

Stamens grow around the stigma. At the end of each stamen is an anther. Anthers contain pollen. Insects and birds help the pollen to travel from flower to flower. The wind also blows the pollen from the anther to other plants of the same species.

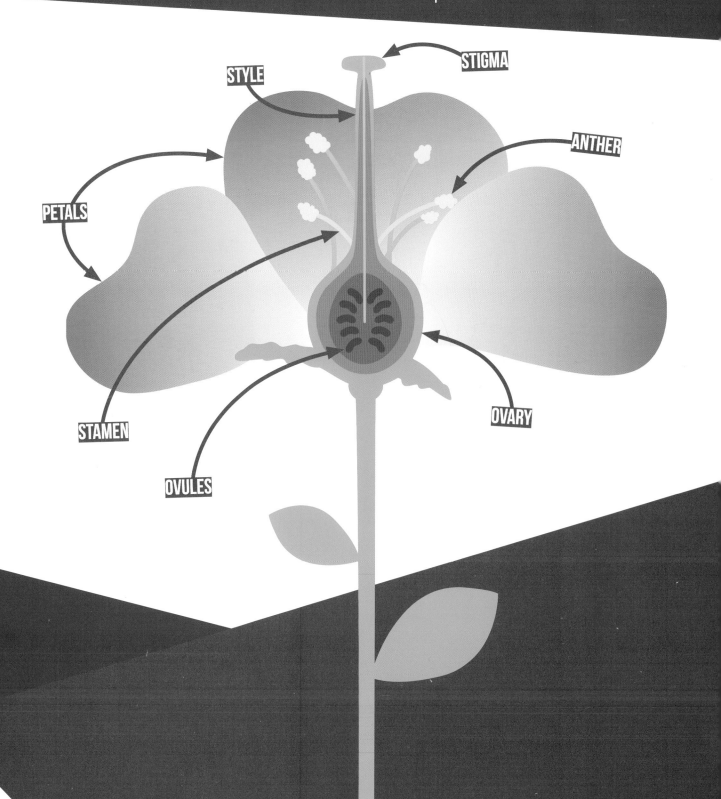

EDIBLE FLOWERS

There are some flowers that humans can safely eat. Broccoli and cauliflower are possibly the most common flowers to be found on a dinner plate. Other flowers are also used to make food items, for example chamomile is used to make tea and sunflowers can be used to make cooking oil.

OTHER USES

As some flowers smell sweet, they are often used as ingredients in perfume. Flowers that are nice to look at are often given as gifts and displayed around the home.

THE
FRUIT

Once a flower has been fertilised, it dies. In its place, a fruit grows. When we hear the word 'fruit', we might think of fruit that we can eat, but all flowering plants grow fruit, which may or may not be edible for humans.

Most importantly, a plant's fruit contains its seeds. The fruit acts as protection for the seeds as they grow. Some fruits contain only one seed, whilst others contain many.

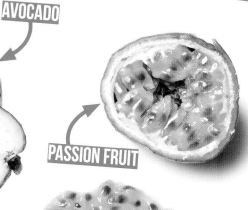

AVOCADO

PASSION FRUIT

PEACH

FLESHY FRUITS

All fruits contain seeds. As with the other plant parts, fruits can come in many different shapes and sizes. The fruits that are tastiest to humans are fleshy fruits. Fleshy fruits have a soft, protective layer around the seeds. Apples, cherries and raspberries are all examples of fleshy fruits.

CHERRIES AND RASPBERRIES

DRY FRUITS

Dry fruits do not have fleshy insides. They split open in order for the seeds to be released. Peas are seeds that come from a dry fruit. In this instance, we eat the seeds more often than the fruit.

A SEED CAPSULE, LIKE THIS ONE FROM A HORSE CHESTNUT TREE, IS A TYPE OF DRY FRUIT.

23

THE ROLE OF FRUIT

Fruits are designed in a specific way so that they protect the plant's seeds whilst they grow, but also so that they are able to move the seed away from the plant in the hope that it will grow elsewhere. This is called seed dispersal (see page 27).

CASE STUDY: AN APPLE

Think about the shape of an apple; it is a sphere. When an apple is ripe, it falls from the tree and the shape of it allows it to roll away. The flesh of the apple is either eaten by an animal or else rots away, leaving the seeds on new ground away from the original tree.

EDIBLE FRUIT

There are many fruits that humans can eat. We tend to think of fruit as being sweet and not savoury, but any plant parts which contain seeds are fruits, therefore many of the vegetables that we eat are fruits too. 'Fruit' is a scientific term, whereas 'vegetable' is more of a cooking term. Vegetables can come from all different parts of a plant.

VEGETABLE FRUIT

Which vegetables do you eat that contain seeds? Cucumbers, courgettes, aubergines, pumpkins, runner beans and tomatoes are all actually fruits!

AUBERGINES

RUNNER BEANS

CUCUMBER

TOMATOES

PUMPKIN

THE SEEDS

Seeds are needed to complete the life cycle of a plant. A plant makes seeds in order for new plants to be able to grow. All plants die, some living longer than others, and so new plants ensure that a plant species will not become **extinct**.

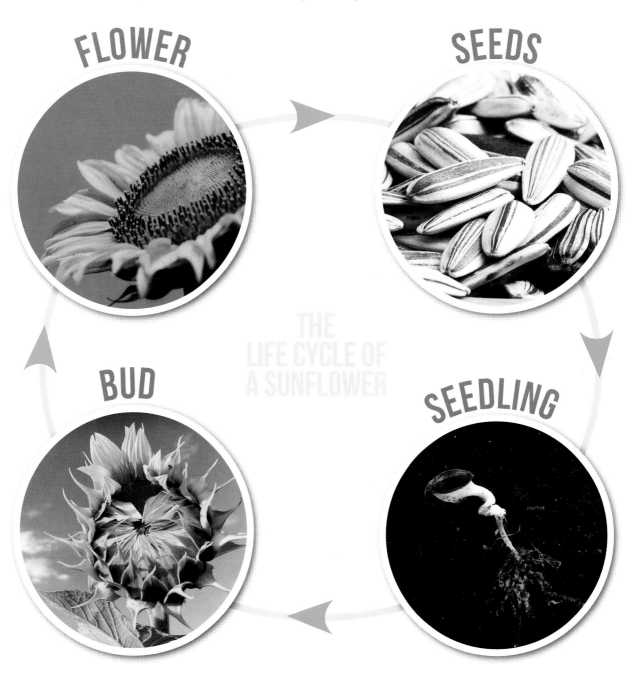

FLOWER

SEEDS

THE LIFE CYCLE OF A SUNFLOWER

BUD

SEEDLING

Most plants make many seeds. In nature, most seeds will not have the correct conditions they need to grow and very few will go on to grow into an adult plant. Plants create many seeds in order to improve their chances of survival.

SEED DISPERSAL

On page 24, we considered one method of seed dispersal, but there are many others. Seed dispersal is very important; if a seed stays too close to the parent plant from which it came, it has less chance of growing.

One of the most important things for any plant is the sun. Plants cannot grow without the light and warmth of the sun. If a seed falls too close to its parent plant, it has to share its resources, including access to the sun. The **established** plant will naturally do better than the seed.

THE SIZE OF THESE ESTABLISHED PLANTS WOULD BLOCK OUT THE SUNLIGHT FOR A SMALL SEED

SEED DISPERSAL USING ANIMALS

Animals can help the dispersal process. They may eat the fruit of a plant but not the seeds, leaving the seeds to grow. Alternatively they may eat the seeds, but, as the seeds are not **digested**, the seeds come out unharmed in the animal's faeces (poo) and can still grow.

Another way in which they might help to move the seeds away is on their coats. Some fruits are designed to hook onto an animal's fur, eventually falling off in a new place.

THE SPIKES OF THIS BURDOCK FRUIT STICK TO FUR.

SEED DISPERSAL USING WIND

Other fruits rely on wind to transport their seeds. These fruits are specifically designed and shaped to do this. The sycamore fruit spins its seeds away from the parent plant like a helicopter. A dandelion seed is attached to a fruit shaped like a parachute.

DANDELION SEEDS

SYCAMORE SEEDS

COCONUT TREES

SEED DISPERSAL USING WATER

Some plants grow close to water. This means that they can use the water to carry away their seeds. Coconut trees often use this method. The seeds float away, eventually stopping on a new patch of land.

EDIBLE SEEDS

As with all parts of a plant, there are some tasty seeds that humans eat. Beans are types of seeds and are often eaten as part of a main meal. Peas and sweetcorn are also the seeds of plants, as are sesame seeds, which can be sprinkled on top of bread rolls.

HUMANS USING SEEDS

Some seeds are prepared before they are eaten. The seeds of cereal grains can be ground down to make flour. Oils **obtained** from some seeds are used for cooking. Many gardeners buy seeds so that they can grow specific plants in their gardens.

GLOSSARY

absorb	take in or soak up
atmosphere	air around us
complex	complicated
digested	to have broken down food that has been absorbed and used by a human's or animal's body
dominant	strongest
established	something that has existed for a long time
extinct	a species that is no longer living
fertilise	cause an egg to develop into a new living thing
obtained	collected
oxygen	a gas in the air which humans need to breathe
perish	die
pillar	a supportive structure
pulp	a soft, wet material
reproduce	make more of the same
sustain	keep alive
transported	moved around
varying	differing

INDEX